W9-APG-260

TERRORIST ATTACKS

ANTHRAX ATTACKS AROUND THE WORLD

Tahara Hasan

The Rosen Publishing Group, Inc.
New York

Published in 2003 by The Rosen Publishing Group, Inc.
29 East 21st Street, New York, NY 10010

Copyright © 2003 by The Rosen Publishing Group, Inc.

First Edition

Library of Congress Cataloging-in-Publication Data

Hasan, Tahara.
Anthrax attacks around the world/by Tahara Hasan.—1st ed.
    p. cm—(Terrorist attacks)
ISBN 0-8239-3859-X (library binding)
1. Anthrax—War use—Juvenile literature. 2. Biological warfare—Juvenile literature. 3. Bioterrorism—Juvenile literature. 4. World politics—1945—Juvenile literature.
I. Title. II. Series.
UG447.8 .H374 2003
303.6'25—dc21

2002011282

Manufactured in the United States of America

CONTENTS

INTRODUCTION

The use of bacteria and viruses in warfare is not new. For years, terrorists and military leaders around the world have used germ and biological elements as weapons to threaten, injure, and kill people. These weapons created from bacteria and viruses are easy and cheap to produce. They are also inexpensive to purchase. This makes biological weapons an ideal choice for terrorists.

Since the terrorist attacks of September 11, 2001, in New York City and Washington, D.C., one biological weapon has received a lot of attention: anthrax. The anthrax disease is one of the most popular weapons used in biological warfare. Anthrax is caused by the bacterium *bacillus anthracis*, which can be found in most of the world's environments. Throughout history, anthrax has been common to farming areas and agricultural life. It has been carried by grass-eating animals that have hooves, such as sheep, cows, goats, and antelope in South America, Asia, Africa, and sections of Europe. Animals can get the disease by drinking water that is near land that has been infected by anthrax. They

An elephant lies in agony after drinking water infected with anthrax in Etosha, Namibia. Although elephants are large, strong animals, generally weighing between 6,600 and 13,200 pounds (3,000 and 6,000 kilograms) and living to the age of seventy, this elephant died only twenty minutes after being exposed to the deadly bacteria.

can also get it by eating dead animals that were infected with the disease.

While it is more commonly found in animals, anthrax can also infect humans when they are exposed to animals or animal parts that have been infected. The first recorded case of anthrax dates back to 1500 BC in Egypt. It was responsible for the fifth Egyptian plague. Later, from AD 500–1500 during the Middle Ages, anthrax killed almost all of the cattle in Europe.

Anthrax has been used as a weapon for years since the bacterium was first recognized by scientists. During World War I (1914–1918), Germany supported secret

Chinese protesters chant anti-Japanese slogans outside of the Tokyo district court on December 25, 2001. They are protesting the Japanese government's treatment of Chinese victims of biological attacks.

attempts to infect livestock with anthrax and sell it to the Allied forces, which included Great Britain, France, and the United States. In 1925, 108 nations, including the United States, Great Britain, France, the Soviet Union, and China signed the Geneva Protocol. This was an agreement by the nations involved to ban the use of biological agents. However, there was no way to ensure that the nations would follow this ban.

During World War II (1939–1945), the Japanese Imperial Army ran a secret biological warfare lab called Unit 731. The Japanese wanted to record the development of various diseases in humans. At Unit 731, they ran experiments on more than 3,000 Chinese prisoners in Manchuria. The victims were exposed to many different diseases, including anthrax.

In 1942 the United States formed the War Research Service, which researched the use of diseases such as anthrax as weapons. Enough anthrax was stored by 1944 in case the Germans decided to use biological weapons during the war.

In 1969 President Richard Nixon ordered the United States to break down its biological weapons programs. The U.S. military had been conducting tests for more than twenty years in the open-air from Minneapolis, Minnesota, to San Francisco, California. The military was trying to learn how clouds of bacteria would travel and decay in the environment in case the United States ever decided to attack the Soviet Union. The programs were broken up or reorganized for peaceful or protective defensive uses.

In 1972 Nixon declared that the United States would support a British plan for an international treaty to ban biological weapons. The Biological Weapons Convention (BWC) was formed. Nations such as the United States, Great Britain, and the Soviet Union were members of the convention.

The BWC bans the making or storing of biological agents that would be used for anything but peaceful reasons. The agreement among the nations was a "good-faith" pact, meaning that participating countries would have to trust one another to keep the promise to stop making biological weapons. While more than one hundred nations signed the treaty, it is not believed that any nation has really stopped making biological weapons.

The United States is not usually prone to anthrax outbreaks. With the world on alert for terrorist attacks today, however, most people are aware of the threat of a possible anthrax attack.

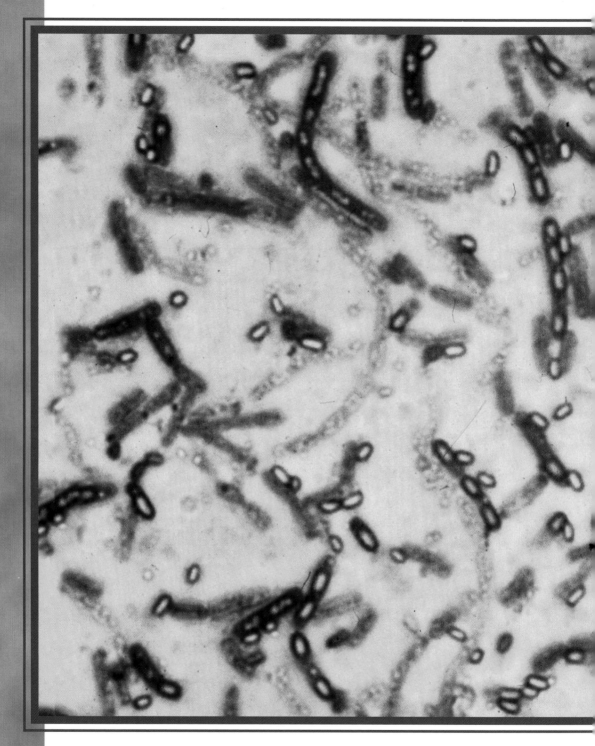

Invisible to the naked eye, anthrax spores can survive for decades thanks to a thick outer coating. Dormant (inactive) anthrax can still be transmitted to humans through ingestion, inhalation, or skin contact.

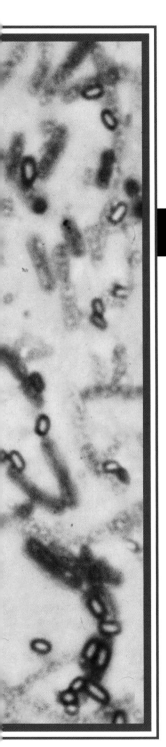

WHAT IS ANTHRAX?

Anthrax is one of the oldest diseases known to humankind. *Bacillus anthracis* was discovered in 1850 by French scientist Casimir-Joseph Davaine, who identified the bacteria when looking at the blood of an infected sheep under a microscope. *Bacillus anthracis* was the first bacterium known to cause a disease. Robert Koch, a German scientist, injected a mouse with *bacillus anthracis* spores to show that when infected with the anthrax bacteria, the mouse died. Ten years later, French microbiologist Louis Pasteur developed a form of anthrax vaccine. A vaccine works by injecting a person with a very small amount of the bacteria—an amount so tiny that the infection will not cause any harm. The person's body will then develop immunity to the disease. This means that the person cannot be infected with the disease again.

Bacillus anthracis can live in the soil for many years in spore form. Spores are tiny, specialized structures that can grow into organisms. Almost every plant and certain kinds of bacteria form spores. Humans can become infected with the anthrax disease by touching products that come from animals infected with anthrax or by inhaling spores from animal products that are contaminated. Veterinarians are able to tell if an animal has died from anthrax by examining its blood. The blood of an infected animal can spill from the animal into the soil. Then, depending on the temperature and the conditions of the blood and the soil, anthrax spores can form.

The Three Types of Anthrax

In human beings, an anthrax infection can start in three different ways. The bacteria can cause a skin infection, an intestinal infection, or an inhalation infection. The skin infection is known as cutaneous anthrax and is the most common form of anthrax. It is also the most treatable, since the symptoms can be easily recognized. Infections can occur if a cut or sore on the skin comes in contact with anthrax. This can happen through the handling of animal products such as wool, leather, or animal hides that have been contaminated by anthrax. However, anthrax is not communicable. This means that it can not be transferred from one person to another.

When a person is infected with cutaneous anthrax, the first symptom to occur is itching. The infected area resembles an insect bite and can appear on the head, arms, or hands. After one or two days, the painless bump will develop a small black center. This is known as an ulcer. Large doses of antibiotics can treat cutaneous anthrax. An antibiotic is a medicine that stops the growth of or destroys microorganisms. If untreated, the cutaneous anthrax infection can spread and cause blood poisoning. The death rate of untreated cutaneous anthrax cases is 20 percent. When a person infected with cutaneous anthrax is treated with antibiotics, however, death is very rare.

The second type of the disease is intestinal anthrax. This is a very rare form of food poisoning that can occur after eating contaminated meat. Intestinal anthrax occurs more commonly in developing nations where meat inspection and vaccination programs are not in place or are ineffective. Symptoms include nausea, loss of appetite, vomiting, fever, stomach pain, and diarrhea. Difficulty breathing and skin infections can also occur. This form of anthrax is hard to recognize. Once a person is diagnosed with intestinal anthrax, treatment consists of heavy doses of antibiotics. The death rate of untreated intestinal anthrax cases is 25 percent to 60 percent.

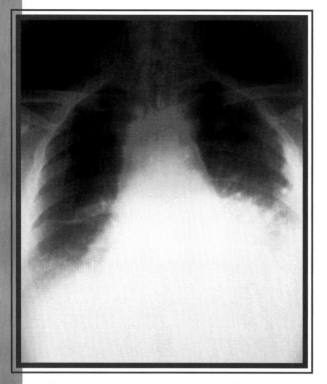

The red area on this computer-enhanced X ray shows an infection of inhalation anthrax. Inhalation is an especially deadly form of the disease that produces lethal toxins that damage the lungs of the afflicted.

The third type, inhalation anthrax, is the most fatal form of the disease. Due to its deadly nature, it is the type of anthrax most likely to be used by terrorists.

Inhalation anthrax is caused when tiny airborne spores of the anthrax disease are inhaled into the mouth, throat, and lungs. The first symptoms of inhalation anthrax are very mild. They often resemble cold or flu symptoms, such as tiredness, fever, cough, or chest pain. At first, there might be a brief period when the symptoms stop. This is known as a false recovery.

The second phase of inhalation anthrax begins after a few days. It consists of high fever, chest or abdominal pain, difficulty breathing, dizziness, vomiting of blood, and diarrhea. Once the spores enter the lungs, they change into poisonous bacteria. The poisonous bacteria are carried throughout the body by the bloodstream. Once this happens, breathing becomes more and more difficult as the disease progresses. Ultimately, the body enters a state of shock. Shock is a very dangerous condition that can occur if blood fails to circulate properly in the body. The toxins in the blood will cause bleeding in the lungs first and then in the liver, kidneys, and stomach. Once the symptoms of inhalation anthrax have started, they are practically untreatable. Shortly afterward, most infected people die.

Treatment

The main treatment for anthrax is antibiotics. Penicillin and tetracycline are two examples of antibiotics that are successful in treating most types of anthrax. They are also inexpensive and easy to obtain because they are produced by many pharmaceutical companies. The antibiotic called Ciproflaxcin has proven to be effective against all forms of anthrax. The only form of Ciproflaxcin that is available in the United States is Cipro. The drug company Bayer holds the exclusive rights to produce Cipro but is working to allow other companies to begin manufacturing the drug.

A vaccine for anthrax does exist. It is reported to be 93 percent effective. The vaccine consists of a harmless part of the bacteria, which is injected into the human body. The body then detects the bacteria and recognizes it as an intruder. It sends antibodies to attack the bacteria.

Ranches all over the country struggle against the spread of anthrax. This farmworker loads up a syringe with an anthrax vaccine to inject into a cow.

Drugs and medicines can be patented like any other invention. When the U.S. government was worried that there would be many anthrax attacks in the United States, they asked Bayer AG, the manufacturers of Cipro, to relax their patent on the product.

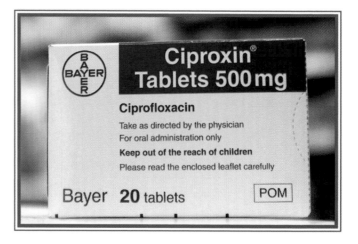

Antibodies are cells that fight infection or disease. Once antibodies have fought the harmless anthrax, they are ready to fight off the more dangerous types of the disease.

In 1970, the U.S. Food and Drug Administration (FDA) approved the anthrax vaccine. However, it is not commercially available in the United States. Those who work in high-risk jobs are advised to get the vaccine. High-risk jobs include:

- People who work with anthrax in a laboratory.

- People who import animal hides or products from areas where health standards are insufficient to prevent exposure to anthrax spores.

- People who handle animal products in regions where anthrax is common.

- Military personnel.

In 1988 a plan was approved to vaccinate all U.S. military personnel against anthrax. However, there have been reports of harmful side effects from anthrax vaccinations given to military personnel during the Persian Gulf War. These side effects include muscle aches, joint aches, headaches, rashes, chills, low-grade fever, and nausea.

Lidia Tretyakova visits the grave of her father, Lazar Karsayev, who was killed in a mysterious anthrax outbreak in 1979 in Sverdlovsk, Russia. At the time, the government concealed the fact that the deaths were due to biological weapons research in the area.

ANTHRAX AND THE SOVIET UNION

The Soviet Union experienced one of history's worst anthrax epidemics in 1979. For many years, it was believed that the outbreak was caused by contaminated meat. It was later discovered, however, to be the result of biological weapons research.

Explosion

In April 1979, the world began to learn of the Soviet Union's biological weapons program. An explosion occurred at a secret military base in the Soviet city of Sverdlovsk, now known as Yekaterinburg. The industrial complex at the military base, Compound 19, was responsible for building rockets, tanks, and other weapons. The explosion released a cloud of deadly spores over a village that was near the military base. At first, authorities believed that 1,000 people had died from inhalation anthrax. The death toll was later changed to approximately sixty-eight people, according to most reports.

A German newspaper released an article about the explosion in October 1979, but a more specific report was given in April 1980. By then, the United States was actively involved in investigating the accident in Sverdlovsk. While the U.S. Department of State announced findings that a biological agent had been released into the atmosphere as a result of this explosion, the Soviet Union claimed that the outbreak was intestinal anthrax caused by contaminated meat. They also said that the accusations were a result of the United States's anti-Soviet feelings.

It was hard to determine which report was accurate. American experts and analysts brought together by U.S. president Jimmy Carter's administration had photos taken by a satellite of Sverdlovsk and the surrounding area. The photos showed the cloud of anthrax spores that was released from the explosion. Some residents of Sverdlovsk had died after inhaling the deadly spores. Some had become sick a few weeks later after eating meat from cattle that had been infected with the disease. The epidemic had gone on for seven weeks. The president's group was then trying to prove that the disease first arrived by inhalation and then by eating infected meat.

One of many spy satellite photos taken of Sverdlovsk, Russia, during the Cold War. This picture is of a uranium-enrichment facility. Conventional, nuclear, and biological weapons were all manufactured in Sverdlovsk during the Cold War.

The Experts

The Central Intelligence Agency (CIA) had called expert Matthew Meselson to help determine the true cause of the anthrax outbreak. Meselson was a Harvard biologist and a major supporter of President Nixon's ban on biological weapons. His experience as an army consultant and scientist made him a good candidate to assist President Carter's group of experts with their research. Meselson had agreed with the group's explanation that the outbreak was caused by the explosion, but he wanted evidence to prove it. This evidence could not be found. Thus, in May 1989, Meselson declared that the anthrax outbreak was the result of poor meat inspection.

Animals infected with anthrax were not kept out of the public meat market. He concluded that an explosion at a biological weapons factory did not cause the anthrax outbreak, as the United States first believed. Meselson even said that he thought the ban on biological weapons was very successful.

However, in October 1989, Soviet biologist Vladimir Pasechnik defected to Great Britain. Pasechnik had directed the Institute for Ultra-Pure Biological Preparations in Leningrad. This institute was just one of the fake fronts for biological weapons research in the Soviet Union. Pasechnik told investigators that the Soviets had a top-secret operation, where thousands of biological specialists were working to master the production and use of germ weapons. This included long-range missiles that were able to spray and spread clouds of germs. Pasechnik revealed that Soviet scientists had combined old and new ways of producing biological weapons to make a brand new type of germ weapon. This new germ weapon had been stored in bombs, rocket warheads, and other weapons. He also told investigators that the new type of biological weapon was only one of many. This information opened the door to uncovering the truth about the anthrax outbreak at Sverdlovsk.

Progress and a Conclusion

By 1992 the Soviet Union had collapsed. Russian leaders had begun to work with American and British officials to uncover the secrets of the past. At a summit at Camp David in Maryland,

Russian president Boris Yeltsin told President George H. W. Bush that Soviet authorities had not been truthful in telling their infected meat story. He even revealed that some members of the Russian military were withholding important information from Yeltsin and his aides about their germ warfare program. Then, on May 27, 1992, Yeltsin publicly stated that

Yeltsin admitted that Russia's 1979 anthrax leak could be traced to a military facility—a worker had forgotten to replace a filter on an exhaust vent.

the 1979 anthrax outbreak was, in fact, the result of an accident at a military complex that had been conducting biological weapons research.

A few days later, Matthew Meselson arrived in Russia. He was in charge of a scientific team called to investigate the Sverdlovsk accident for a second time and to gather evidence. With greater access and cooperation from the Russians, the team was able to interview health officials and family members of the people who died from the anthrax outbreak. The Russian health officials showed the team slides and X rays of the victims' lungs, the organ most affected by inhalation anthrax. Indeed, the evidence showed signs of damage from inhalation anthrax rather than intestinal anthrax.

Kanatjan Alibekov was a Russian scientist who also defected to the United States; he changed his name to Ken Alibek because it sounded more American. Like Vladimir Pasechnik, he had important information to share with American investigators. Alibek spoke mainly with Bill Patrick, who had been in charge of biological weapons development at Fort Detrick, the U.S. Army base for research and production of germ weapons. Patrick was considered an expert on germ warfare. Even when he no longer worked at Fort Detrick, he was brought in because of his great knowledge of biological weapons. Alibek told Patrick that the Soviets had produced tons of anthrax, plague, and smallpox germs. The germs were stored for use against the United States and its allies.

Alibek also revealed that the Soviet Academy of Sciences and the Ministries of Defense and Agriculture were all involved in the secret production of biological weapons. Alibek was able to tell Patrick about other scientific germ work that the Soviets had been conducting since the 1970s. Compound 19 was the Soviet Union's most active germ-making facility. Scientists there worked almost nonstop to produce anthrax and other germs.

In 1994 Matthew Meselson and his team gave their final conclusions on the anthrax outbreak in Sverdlovsk. This time Meselson was able to prove that spores, leaked from a military facility at Sverdlovsk, caused the outbreak. The tiny amount of anthrax that had leaked, a little less than a gram, was actually quite potent. The team had data on wind directions and the locations of seventy-nine cases at the time of the explosion. This information was the last bit needed to prove that inhalation of anthrax spores caused the deaths at Sverdlovsk. It confirmed that the Soviets had been creating a germ arsenal that could have devastated the United States.

Stepnogorsk

The information discovered about Sverdlovsk was not all that the U.S. government learned about Russia and germ warfare. In 1982 the Scientific Experimental and Production Base, known as Stepnogorsk was built in the Soviet Union. This factory was a part of the Soviet biological warfare production plan. Its mission was to create the most lethal version of anthrax ever. Inside the facility, the equipment used to create anthrax could fill a field more than 200 yards (182.9 meters) long, the length of two football fields. The facility could produce 300 tons of anthrax spores in approximately 220 days.

The amount of anthrax produced at Stepnogorsk was enough to wipe out the U.S. population. At least six other production facilities like Stepnogorsk existed that were part of a germ plan of secret cities and centers that researched and produced biological weapons. More than 30,000 people were employed in one of these germ facilities. The Soviet

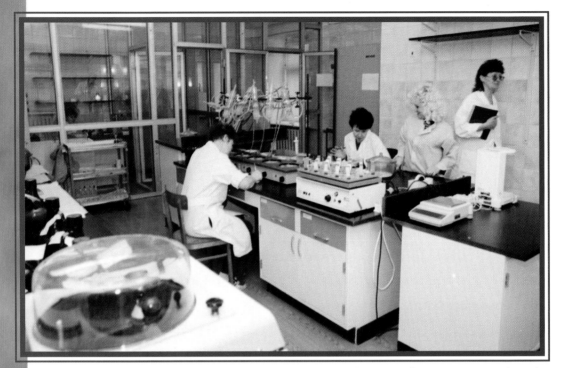

Scientists conduct experiments in the Stepnogorsk Scientific Experimental and Production Base, a building that was once the biggest anthrax manufacturing plant in the world.

military ran the biological weapons program. They had more than $1 billion a year to spend on research, production, and the storing of anthrax and other biological weapons to be used in missiles and bombs. The Soviets called these germs "product."

Obtaining evidence of Soviet production of biological weapons at Stepnogorsk was much easier than finding evidence of biological weapons at Sverdlovsk. Most of the equipment used to make the weapons was still intact. Scientists and authorities revealed that the Stepnogorsk facility had made the most powerful strains of anthrax ever. A strain is a specified group that shares characteristics or qualities. Some were even resistant to antibiotics. The most powerful of all the strains was No. 836. It was created by Ken Alibek, and it was called Alibekov anthrax. What made the strain so powerful was the fact that it needed fewer spores to become an effective weapon. It was three times as powerful as the version leaked at Sverdlovsk in 1979.

With the fall of the Soviet Union in 1991, the United States was able to send more researchers into Russia to investigate anthrax cases. They learned that in 1988 Soviet scientists had been ordered to get rid of the anthrax bacteria it had produced and stored. It was another piece of evidence revealing that the Soviet Union had broken the treaty of the 1972 Biological Weapons Convention. The Soviets had disposed of the germs at Renaissance Island, the former designated area for germ tests in the Soviet Union. They poured bleach into the storage containers that contained anthrax to contaminate it. Then they dug holes and buried the mixture of anthrax and bleach, in order to hide the evidence that the Soviets had broken the germ treaty.

While the collapse of the Soviet Union had provided an opportunity for the Soviets' secrets to be uncovered, there was also a negative side. When the Soviet Union dissolved, many Russian scientists lost their jobs and could have considered selling their germ secrets to countries that were also likely to attack the United States. In addition, anonymous individuals could also obtain information needed to make the new, more powerful biological weapons. This made the threat of germ warfare even more possible against the United States.

Japanese police seize hundreds of drums containing chemicals used to make nerve gas from an Aum Shinrikyo cult commune on March 25, 1995. Cult members watch from the window above.

THE AUM SHINRIKYO CULT

In the 1990s, Japan was dealing with its own form of terrorism. A cult was working to produce biological weapons and use them against citizens of Japan. Between 1990 and 1995, this cult engaged in several failed attempts at terrorism. However, in late March 1995, the cult successfully killed twelve Tokyo citizens and terrorized and injured thousands of others in a biological attack.

Shoko Asahara

The Aum Shinrikyo cult was started in the late 1980s by Shoko Asahara, a man who claimed to have supernatural powers. He believed that he was a messiah,

This image from a Japanese news program shows Shoko Asahara, leader of the Aum Shinrikyo cult, proclaiming his innocence to reporters.

someone who is viewed as a savior by his or her followers. He saw himself as leading his followers to safety as the end of the world came closer. Asahara wanted to bring about a worldwide conflict using biological, chemical, and nuclear weapons to destroy Japan. He believed that he and anyone who believed in his power could survive such an end to the world. The cult believed in mass killing to further its beliefs.

The cult had anywhere from 20,000 to 40,000 members all over the world. It was able to raise money through the donations of its members. Aum Shinrikyo also raised funds by selling religious memorabilia, videos, and books. It charged members for induction courses on the teachings of the cult. These courses could cost anywhere from hundreds to thousands of dollars. In addition, the cult owned a chain of restaurants in a few Japanese cities. By 1995, the Aum Shinrikyo cult had assets of more than $1 billion.

THE RAJNEESHEE CULT

In 1984, the United States experienced its first large-scale act of biological terrorism, or bioterrorism. The Rajneeshees, a religious cult that formed in Antelope, Oregon, planned to poison people in their county in order to win a political election and, ultimately, control of the county. First, they brought homeless people from around the country into their group and registered them to vote in Oregon. The goal was to have the homeless vote for Rajneeshee officials. The second part of the plan was to physically weaken supporters of their political opponents so they could not make it to the polls to vote. County officials grew suspicious, however, of the large number of newly registered voters and demanded that a special panel question all new voters.

The Rajneeshees began to carry out their plan to poison voters by contaminating salad bars at restaurants in the nearby community of The Dalles. They used salmonella, a common bacteria causing food poisoning when consumed. At least 750 county residents fell ill with salmonella poisoning in the fall of 1984. Upon investigation of the Rajneeshee medical lab, town health officials discovered vials that contained salmonella. The samples taken matched the strain of salmonella that had made the townspeople violently ill. However, it wasn't until a year after the salmonella outbreak that it was proven that the Rajneeshees had committed an act of bioterrorism. This happened after some cult members confessed their wrongdoings.

Although the incident was the first large-scale use of germs in a terrorist attack in the United States, public health officials did not publicize the event. They were concerned that copycat attacks might occur as a result of such publicity.

Police guard a house belonging to the Aum Shinrikyo cult. Surrounded with fences, barbed wire, and trenches, it is 87 miles (140 kilometers) outside of Tokyo.

From 1990 to 1995, the Aum Shinrikyo cult attempted at least a dozen unsuccessful biological attacks in Japan. Some of these attacks involved anthrax. In 1993 the cult tried a mass killing by spraying anthrax spores from a rooftop. The cult had occupied an eight-story building in a suburb of Tokyo. Cult members built towers on top of the building and sprayed fluid containing the deadly anthrax spores. When this failed, the cult tried again by driving through Tokyo, releasing spores through truck vents. Again, this did not kill anybody.

The building had a foul odor that caused a number of public complaints. When investigators inspected the building to determine the exact nature of the odor, they took samples of a fluid present on the walls and sent them to a laboratory at Northern Arizona University for analysis. Scientists confirmed that the samples contained anthrax. Since anthrax is odorless, the scientists believed that the smell came from the ingredients used to make the liquid anthrax. Through their studies, they also learned that the anthrax was a strain used in veterinary vaccines for cattle. It would not kill humans. Scientists reported that even if the cult had tried to spread anthrax through a powder form instead of a liquid form, the size of the spores created were not large enough to cause any damage.

BIOLOGICAL WEAPONS INVENTORY

Many biological agents can be used to create weapons. Some of the biological weapons developed by countries around the world include:

Botulism A toxin known to be the most poisonous existing compound, it paralyzes the muscles and then prevents breathing, which then results in a quick death.

Q Fever A mild disease that causes chills, coughing, headaches, hallucinations, and fevers up to 104° F (40° C).

Sarin A liquid chemical that is odorless and colorless; it shuts down the body's central nervous system and can be deadly if inhaled.

Smallpox A disease whose initial symptoms are high fever, fatigue, headaches, and backaches; a rash follows and then lesions develop. Smallpox is most contagious during the first week of illness. There is no proven treatment. Currently, the United States has an emergency supply of the smallpox vaccine, which has proven successful.

Tularemia A disease that causes chills, fever, and coughing as well as very large skin ulcers up to an inch wide; antibiotics will not weaken it; very few treatments exist, except for immunization.

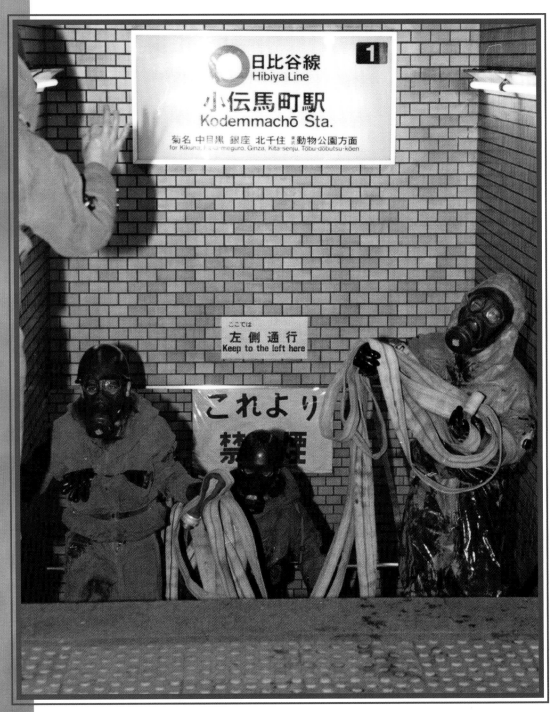

Japanese firemen emerge from the Kodemmacho subway station after cleaning contaminated subway cars following the Aum Shinrikyo nerve gas attacks.

There were a few theories about why the Aum Shinrikyo cult chose a strain of anthrax normally used for livestock vaccines. One theory was that the cult simply did not know the anthrax was from a vaccine strain and thought that it would kill people. A second was that the version that the cult used was only a test run for when they used the actual strain that would be able to kill. Another theory was that a member of the cult changed his mind and had switched the strain of anthrax that was to be used. Finally, some experts believed that the members were under too much pressure from their cult leader, Asahara, and carried through their biological attack even though they knew it would fail.

A Successful Attack

In 1995 the Aum Shinrikyo cult succeeded in carrying out a bioterrorism attack. The cult released the nerve gas sarin into a Tokyo subway. Twelve people were killed and many others were injured. Until this attack, not many countries knew about Aum Shinrikyo. As the United States investigated the history and actions of the cult, they learned that as early as 1993, the group had tried to purchase equipment that was used for making nuclear bombs. The United States took an active role in investigating the Aum Shinrikyo cult in order to learn how to prepare for and prevent bioterrorist attacks.

Young boys brandish AK-47 assault rifles at a military base in Baghdad during Iraq's 1990 occupation of Kuwait. UN troops fought the Iraqi army in an effort to end the occupation during Operation Desert Storm.

ANTHRAX AND IRAQ

CHAPTER

T he United States had good reason to worry about biological warfare prior to Aum Shinrikyo's attack in Japan. On August 2, 1990, Iraqi leader Saddam Hussein ordered his army to invade Kuwait, a small country that borders Iraq. The United States sent military troops to this region, known as the Persian Gulf. At home, scientists were conducting experiments to find out what would be the best medical defense against an anthrax attack. The United States believed that Saddam Hussein had a large supply of germ weapons. Even though they were aware of the events at Sverdlovsk, the United States was not prepared to deal with biological warfare. American soldiers had not been protected against any type of germ threat. This made the possibility of anthrax even more deadly, since treatment is highly ineffective after the first symptoms of inhalation anthrax appear. Scientists at Fort Detrick worked day and night to discover possible treatments against anthrax.

Project Badger

General Norman Schwarzkopf was in charge of the U.S. military's Central Command (CENTCOM). This department was responsible for defending the Persian Gulf. Days after the Iraqi invasion of Kuwait, Schwarzkopf sent hundreds of thousands of American troops to Saudi Arabia, one of Kuwait's neighbors. Its position was vital to the American defense. Schwarzkopf's biggest worry was protecting his troops from an anthrax attack. Although antibiotics were available, the technology needed to test for anthrax spores in the atmosphere at an early stage was not yet available. The United Nations (UN) had given Iraq a deadline of January 15, 1991, to withdraw from Kuwait. The United States desperately needed to develop their technology to detect airborne anthrax spores before that deadline.

On August 20, 1990, U.S. government health officials put together a group of doctors, intelligence experts, and military officers. The group's name was the Ad Hoc

U.S. general Norman Schwarzkopf jokes with the soldiers of the 1st Infantry Division in Saudi Arabia. Schwarzkopf was made a five-star general for his leadership during Operation Desert Storm.

Group for the Medical Defense against Biological Warfare. It was later renamed Project Badger because one of the participating doctors recalled that anthrax could be transferred through everyday items such as shaving brushes. Some of the best shaving brushes were made of badger hairs. Project Badger was responsible for finding the solution to the germ problem. They worked together to study reports of Iraq's germ purchases, specifically its anthrax supply. They had to find out facts such as what kind of anthrax Iraq had and how many soldiers would die if it were released.

A vaccine was developed. Nevertheless, not enough vaccine was available for U.S. troops or U.S. allies. In order to produce enough vaccine, more assembly lines would have to be formed. A very tight schedule would have to be kept during processing, testing, and packaging. Drug companies around the United States were asked to produce more vaccines. Many did not want to be involved due to the fact that anthrax spores are lethal and could last in buildings for a very long time. As such, the buildings where the vaccine would be made could not be used for anything else.

The Supply

The U.S. government was still trying to determine specifically what Saddam Hussein had in his biological weapons supply. Experts studied satellite images of Iraqi sites that they suspected contained stores of anthrax and other germ warfare products. They also listened to bits and pieces of telephone conversations between Iraqi officials and scientists and Western businessmen who sold germ equipment to Iraq.

The U.S. government discovered that Iraq had an equipment and germ supply that would allow them to launch an attack that could cause massive destruction to the Allied Forces. The Iraqi supply of anthrax could easily be released from aerosol sprayers used to distribute pesticides over crops. In 1990 Iraq purchased forty aerosol sprayers from a company

The U.S. 1st Cavalry Division begins a long march across the Saudi Arabian desert to take up strategic positions during the war against Iraq. By the time these ground troops invaded, many of the military's objectives had already been accomplished from the air.

in Italy. Each sprayer could send out 800 gallons of liquid or dry germs per hour. The transport of the sprayers would be easy, too. They could fit on a small boat, a single-engine plane, or the back of a vehicle like a pick-up truck. The American government was not only worried about its own troops but about the lives of civilians in neighboring countries and at home. Saddam Hussein's germ arsenal could also be used in a terrorist attack in the United States.

As the January 15 deadline drew near, experts at the Pentagon realized that even if the first group of soldiers had received their first set of vaccines by December 10, they would not have minimum protection against anthrax until January 21, six days past the deadline. The anthrax vaccine is not effective immediately. Project Badger was using a lab in Michigan to produce more of the anthrax vaccine. It had made enough for a little more than a quarter of the American troops stationed in Saudi Arabia. There was none for the other Allied Forces or for Saudi citizens.

Vaccinations

On December 17, 1990, the chairman of the Joint Chiefs of Staff, General Colin L. Powell, gave his final recommendations on vaccinating the troops to Dick Cheney, the U.S. defense secretary. Powell said that the process of vaccinating should begin immediately. The pair then went to see President George H. W. Bush, who approved the plan to vaccinate troops quickly. On December 29, Powell notified General Schwarzkopf to begin immunization procedures against anthrax and botulism. To put to rest fears that the vaccine was unsafe, General Schwarzkopf received a shot himself. Any soldier who did not want the vaccine could refuse it. Schwarzkopf wanted every soldier who received an injection to read and sign a release form. Vaccinations began in early January, and every soldier was also given enough Cipro antibiotic to last five days. Shortly after the war, Persian Gulf veterans started to complain of symptoms that included

A Tomahawk cruise missile is fired from the USS *Wisconsin* during an attack on Iraq. Tomahawk missiles have a range of up to 1,000 miles (1,600 kilometers).

joint pain and memory loss. Some blamed the anthrax vaccine. Due to poor record keeping, however, it was difficult to verify who had received the injections.

A few months earlier, President Bush and his top security aides were trying to determine what action to take if Iraq carried out a biological attack. They solved this problem by threatening to use nuclear weapons against Iraq if Iraq used germ weapons. It was a well-kept secret, however, that President Bush did not want to use nuclear weapons. If needed, the U.S. military would expand its bombing campaign. The message that Bush sent to Hussein, however, was that the United States would take nuclear revenge if Iraq used anthrax or any other biological weapons.

On January 16, 1991, a day after the UN deadline, Iraq had still not withdrawn from Kuwait. As a result, the United States launched Tomahawk cruise missiles from aircraft carriers in the Persian Gulf. What would follow was the largest bombing campaign in history. Within the first few days of the war, the Iraqi air defenses were demolished. It was also believed that plants where biological weapons were made were destroyed. On February 28, 1991, Iraq surrendered. Iraq's advanced weapons were no match for those of the Allied Forces. Bombs that can be guided by radio waves or a laser beam, called smart bombs, were believed to have hit their targets, and the American Patriot missile defense system was believed to have knocked Iraqi Scud missiles right out of the sky. As far as the American Defense Intelligence Agency knew, it would cost Iraq almost $200 million to rebuild their germ production facilities.

Time would tell a different story, however. The American smart bombs had missed many targets, and the Scud-destroying attacks were not nearly as successful as first reported. In addition, Iraq had a secret storage of germs that was much bigger than anyone had imagined. These germs were kept at many laboratories and buildings that were not destroyed in the bombings.

The Weapons Supply

After the war, Iraq began to prepare to hide its weapons plans from the United Nations. Iraqi officials destroyed documents, created false walls in buildings that held germ weapons, and rehearsed stories that they would tell UN inspectors regarding their germ arsenal. The United Nations formed a committee, called the United Nations Special Commission (UNSCOM), whose job was to see if Iraq's claim of the limited creation of biological weapons was true. At the same time, the CIA was conducting its own investigation.

In May 1991, the CIA received reports that Iraq's biological weapons supply had survived the war. They also found out that the Al-Hakam facility in Iraq had produced germ weapons, and that the Iraqis had buried bombs containing different biological agents near a major military base. The CIA reports also revealed that the Al-Hakam facility had five laboratories that were used to create toxins in very large tanks. By September 1991, the CIA was able to name eight locations in Iraq that were believed to have produced biological weapons. Anthrax was just one of the germs produced at these facilities. The CIA reports held information that the members of UNSCOM did not have.

By the fall of 1991, the CIA had solved the mystery of the Iraqi germ arsenal. One of the germs being produced was anthrax. Iraqi scientists claimed that the facilities and the equipment in them were used to produce animal feed.

A United Nations worker inspects Iraqi rockets filled with sarin, the same deadly nerve gas used by the Aum Shinrikyo cult in Japan. Sarin was only one of the chemicals that UN soldiers came into contact with during the Gulf War.

It wasn't until four years later that UNSCOM discovered the same information. After many trips to Iraq, the committee, lead by Richard Spertzel, a germ expert from Fort Detrick, discovered some important Iraqi files. The files included documents that recorded Iraqi orders for germ supplies used for producing anthrax, including a culture medium. A culture medium is the nutrient material used to grow bacteria. Iraqi engineers were also finally confessing to knowing about the biological weapons facilities, whose existence they had denied all along.

Iraqi technicians had been creating tanks that could spray large amounts of anthrax from a jet. They also said that they had started to experiment with viruses. Shortly before the invasion of Kuwait, they buried the bombs and missiles that contained the biological agents. If used, the aerosol sprayers containing these agents could have caused a massive number of deaths.

On August 8, 1995, Lieutenant General Hussein Kamel, one of Saddam Hussein's sons-in-law, defected to Jordan. He confessed to UNSCOM that Iraq had made large quantities of weapons out of germs. Kamel also acknowledged the conspiracy to hide the biological weapons movement from the United Nations. Finally, the truth was being heard. Documents on Iraq's germ program were suddenly turning up as evidence. This was the breakthrough that UNSCOM needed to prove the scope of Iraq's germ program.

After a letter containing anthrax spores was discovered in the U.S. House of Representatives on October 20, 2001, the Capitol building was completely evacuated.

ANTHRAX TODAY

The latest anthrax news came shortly after the terrorist attacks against the United States on September 11, 2001. The use of four hijacked planes as bombs were the first attacks on American soil in more than fifty years. Suddenly, everyone in the country was aware of the threat to homeland security.

In the days following the brutal attacks, several anthrax-contaminated letters passed through the U.S. postal system. The entire nation was placed on high alert and citizens panicked about possible bioterrorism attacks. The U.S. government had the job of figuring out whether the terrorist attacks and anthrax attacks were masterminded by the same group of terrorists.

Attacks on America

On Tuesday, September 11, 2001, terrorists attacked the United States in several different locations. Three hijacked planes loaded with fuel and carrying passengers and crewmembers were used as bombs, flying into U.S. landmarks. One plane is believed to have been overtaken by its passengers and crashed into a field near

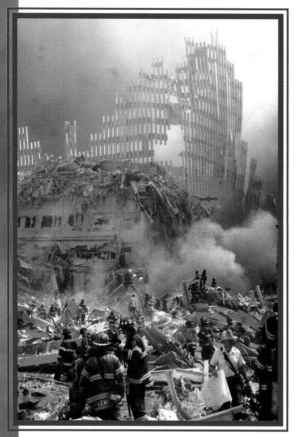

Emergency workers search the rubble of the World Trade Center for survivors following the terrorist attacks on September 11, 2001.

Pittsburgh, Pennsylvania. Thousands of people were killed as a result of these attacks. The number of deaths was the largest that America had experienced at home in an act of terrorism.

The terrorists aboard the four planes were linked to the Al Qaeda terrorism network. The United States has long been the chief enemy of Al Qaeda, an extremist Islamic terrorist organization. The group was founded in the 1980s by Osama bin Laden—someone the U.S. government had known about for a long time.

OSAMA BIN LADEN

A millionaire born in 1957 in Saudi Arabia, Osama bin Laden is one of the most notorious figures in world history. His hatred of the U.S. government has led to more than one terrorist attack. Bin Laden and his followers are responsible for attacks on U.S. embassies in Tanzania and Kenya in 1998, an earlier bombing of the World Trade Center in 1993, and the devastating attacks of September 11, 2001. His anti-Americanism stems from his disapproval of the alliance his native Saudi Arabia had with the U.S. government during the Persian Gulf War. After the attacks on the World Trade Center and the Pentagon, the U.S. military and allied forces began a hunt for bin Laden, who is famously elusive. At the time of this printing, it is not known whether bin Laden is alive or dead.

The Anthrax Outbreak

Shortly after the September 11 attacks, the United States experienced an assault of a different kind. An anthrax outbreak scare occurred in the United States.

On September 25, 2001, NBC television studios received a letter postmarked a few days earlier from Trenton, New Jersey. The letter contained an unidentified white powder. The FBI and other law enforcement officials were immediately notified. The *New York Post* also received a letter contaminated with anthrax around this time. Six

This letter containing anthrax spores was sent to the editor of the *New York Post*; thankfully, no one there was seriously infected. Letters were also sent to Senate majority leader Tom Daschle and news anchor Tom Brokaw.

days later, Erin O'Connor, an assistant to NBC news anchor Tom Brokaw, who handled the letter from Trenton, started to complain of a rash. On October 12, officials announced that she had developed cutaneous anthrax.

On October 2, sixty-three-year-old photo editor Robert Stevens was admitted to a hospital with a very high fever and disorientation. He worked at American Media, Inc., a tabloid publisher in Florida. A day later, it was announced that Stevens had inhalation anthrax. On October 5, Stevens died. His death was the first American anthrax fatality in twenty-five years. American Media closed its offices two days after he died. Investigators discovered anthrax spores on his keyboard. They also found anthrax spores in the nasal passages of seventy-three-year-old Ernesto Blanco, the mailroom supervisor at American Media. Although diagnosed with inhalation anthrax, Blanco was treated and recovered. On October 18, an assistant to CBS news anchor Dan Rather tested positive for cutaneous anthrax. Spores were also found in Dan Rather's office.

Although the terrorists sending the anthrax-laced letters did not kill any of their intended targets, they demonstrated how easily the disease could be distributed through the mail.

Anthrax was making its way into the lives of not only American journalists but politicians as well. On October 15, a letter testing positive for anthrax and postmarked October 9 in Trenton was found in South Dakota senator Tom Daschle's Washington, D.C., office. The newly appointed U.S. Homeland Security Chief, Tom Ridge, reported that the anthrax found in Senator Daschle's letter was of the purest form and highly concentrated. He also revealed that only a small number of countries, including the United States, are believed to be capable of producing the refined anthrax found in the senator's letter.

On October 17, anthrax spores were discovered on New York governor George Pataki's office computer keyboard. Pataki's staff all tested negative for exposure to anthrax, but they began taking Cipro as a precautionary measure. In Washington, D.C., several traces of anthrax were found at the U.S. Supreme Court, the State Department, a Health and Human Services building, and an Agriculture Department office. Officials announced on November 16 that an anthrax letter similar to Senator Daschle's was sent to Vermont senator Patrick Leahy.

Employees at mail processing centers were infected with anthrax, too. In a mail processing center in Trenton, New Jersey, anthrax was found in thirteen locations. Three workers tested positive for anthrax exposure. On October 21, two employees at a Washington, D.C., mail-processing center tested positive for inhalation anthrax. Shortly afterward, two other employees at the center visited their doctors because of respiratory problems. One of the patients died of inhalation anthrax.

Postal workers around the country were given safety lectures. They were told to keep an eye out for anything that looked suspicious or unusual, such as something that had powder on it. Postal workers were also given latex gloves and masks to wear to protect themselves from becoming

Postal workers as far away as São Paolo, Brazil, wore masks and gloves to protect themselves from accidentally contracting anthrax.

infected with anthrax. Postal employees from Trenton, New Jersey, were being carefully monitored for anthrax, since many of the anthrax letters were postmarked in Trenton.

The Investigation

The Federal Bureau of Investigation (FBI) had the difficult task of determining not only the source of the contaminated letters but also the source of the anthrax itself. Agents had to look at many possibilities, including that the individuals responsible for the September 11 terrorist attacks might also be to blame for the anthrax attacks. To make matters worse, many false alarms occurred. As of January 23, 2002, more than 15,000 hoaxes were reported. As a result of the anthrax scare, 540 postal facilities closed temporarily, and seventy-one people were arrested.

The FBI offered a reward of $1.25 million for any information on the anthrax attacks and then doubled it to $2.5 million. They mailed more than 500,000 fliers to New Jersey and Pennsylvania, hoping to receive help from citizens. The fliers pointed out important portions of the anthrax letters that were sent to Senators Daschle and Leahy, Tom Brokaw, and the *New York Post*. The sender's handwriting and the letter's embossed postage stamps were some of the highlighted features. All four of the letters had Trenton, New Jersey, postmarks, so investigators paid close attention to this region.

Many people believed that the terrorist group responsible for the September 11 attacks was responsible for the anthrax attacks. It was also believed that Iraq could have supplied the anthrax used in the letters. The letters contained messages such as "Death to America," "Allah is Great," and "Death to Israel." However, all of the letter samples contained the same strain of anthrax, known as the Ames strain. The Ames strain has been widely used in vaccine studies. It is one of eighty-nine known genetic variations of anthrax and is resistant to many vaccines. The number of labs known to have this strain is no more than twelve.

At the time of the writing of this book, many authorities believe that the anthrax perpetrator could be an American who took advantage of the September 11 chaos and initiated his or her anthrax attacks soon after, so that blame would be placed on Islamic terrorists. Expert hand-writing analysts for the FBI concluded that a Westerner and not a Muslim or someone from the Middle East

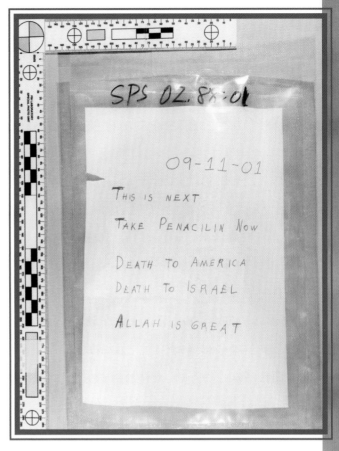

Even a year after the terror-related anthrax outbreaks in the United States, investigators were no closer to discovering the identity of the person or group who sent these letters.

wrote the letters, even though the letters were written to make investigators believe that was the case.

It is believed that the suspect is a middle-aged, white male who has a doctoral degree in biology and is an expert in U.S. biodefense. He is thought to have experience working with hazardous germs, including anthrax. Since the letters were carefully taped and contained warnings of the lethal nature of anthrax and information on antibiotic cures, it is believed that the suspect's motives were not to kill anyone but to spread fear.

Investigators are paying special attention to government biodefense labs such as the U.S. Army Medical Research Institute of Infectious Disease (USAMRIID) at Fort Detrick, Maryland. There have been reports of security breaks, and in the past the institute did not keep records of which labs had what strain of anthrax. In late September 2001, a former USAMRIID scientist of Egyptian descent was accused of being a terrorist. An anonymous letter was sent to the military police at Quantico Marine Base that accused Dr. Ayaad Assaad of being responsible for the anthrax-tainted letters. The FBI questioned Assaad and concluded that he had nothing to do with the attacks. Investigators believe that the suspect may have previously worked at USAMRIID and tried to frame Assaad.

The anthrax mailings in the United States killed five people and infected at least seventeen others. The source of these attacks is still unknown. One thing that is certain is that anthrax is not any single nation's problem. Scientists continue to research it. Countries and terrorists continue to weaponize it. Until humankind can learn to live peacefully, biological weapons such as anthrax will continue to threaten the lives of innocent people.

GLOSSARY

aerosol A substance enclosed under pressure and able to be released as a fine spray.

airborne Transported by air.

bacteria Any group of microscopic organisms that live in soil, water, or the bodies of plants or animals.

biological Relating to plant and animal life.

bioterrorism Terrorist activities involving the use of biological weapons to kill or injure.

contaminate To make something impure by exposure to or addition of a poisonous or polluting substance.

defect To abandon one's country or cause in favor of an opposing one.

facility Space or equipment necessary for performing a certain activity.

germ A microorganism that can cause disease.

immunity The ability of an organism to resist a particular infection or toxin.

induction The process of admitting a person formally to a position or organization.

infection The process of becoming inflicted with a disease-causing organism.

outbreak The sudden or violent start of something unwelcome, such as disease.

pesticide A substance used for destroying insects or other organisms harmful to plants or animals.

spore A single-celled reproductive body that is capable of growing into a new organism.

strain A group of organisms of the same species that have distinctive characteristics but are not usually considered a separate breed or variety.

summit A meeting between heads of government.

terrorist A person who uses violence and intimidation to attain political goals.

toxin A poison of plant or animal origin that can come from microorganisms and can cause disease in the body.

vaccine A substance used to provide immunity against one or several diseases.

warfare The activities of armed conflict between different nations or groups within a nation.

virus The causing element of infectious disease.

FOR MORE INFORMATION

Centers for Disease Control and Prevention (CDC)
1600 Clifton Road
Atlanta, GA 30333
(404) 630-3311
Web site: http://www.cdc.gov

Center for the Study of Bioterrorism and Emerging Infections
St. Louis University School of Public Health
3545 Lafayette, Suite 300
St. Louis, MO 63104
(314) 977-8257
Web site: http://www.bioterrorism.slu.edu

U.S. Department of Defense
Assistant Secretary of Public Affairs
The Pentagon
Washington, DC 20301
Web site: http://www.defenselink.mil

U.S. Department of Health and Human Services
200 Independence Avenue SW
Washington, DC 20201
(201) 619-0257
Web site: http://www.os.dhhs.gov

World Health Organization (WHO)
Avenue Appia 20
1211 Geneva 27
Switzerland
(+00 41 22) 791 2111
Web site: http://www.who.int/home-page

Web Sites

Due to the changing nature of Internet links, the Rosen Publishing Group, Inc., has developed an online list of Web sites related to the subject of this book. This site is updated regularly. Please use this link to access the list:

http://www.rosenlinks.com/ta/aaaw/

FOR FURTHER READING

Alexander, Yonah, and Milton M. Hoenig, eds. *Super Terrorism: Biological, Chemical, and Nuclear.* Ardsley, NY: Transnational Publishers, 2001.

Corvisier, Andre. *A Dictionary of Military History.* Malden, MA: Blackwell, 1994.

Levine, Herbert M. *Chemical and Biological Weapons in Our Time.* Danbury, CT: Franklin Watts, 2000.

Meltzer, Milton, and Sergio Martinez. *Weapons and Warfare: From the Stone Age to the Space Age.* New York: HarperCollins, 1996.

U.S. Department of Defense. *21st Century Bioterrorism and Germ Weapons—U.S. Army Field Manual for the Treatment of Biological Warfare Agent Casualties (Anthrax, Smallpox, Plague, Viral Fevers, Toxins, Delivery Methods, Detection, Symptoms, Treatment, Equipment).* 2001.

BIBLIOGRAPHY

Centers for Disease Control and Prevention Web site. "Anthrax." Retrieved February 2, 2002 (http://www.cdc. gov/ncidod/dbmd/diseaseinfo/anthrax_t.htm).

Centers for Disease Control and Prevention Web site. "Statement by the Department of Health and Human Services." 2001. Retrieved February 2, 2002 (http://www.bt.cdc.gov/documentsapp/anthrax/12182001/ hhs12182001.asp).

Gugliotta, Guy. "Panel Says Anthrax Vaccine Is Safe." *Washington Post*. 2002. Retrieved April 29, 2002 (http://www.washingtonpost.com/ac2/wp-dyn?page-name=article&node=&contentId=A49357-2002Mar6& notFound=true).

Potter, Mark. "Ex-U.N. Weapons Inspector: Possible Iraq-Anthrax Link." CNN.com. Retrieved February 2, 2002 (http://www.cnn.com/ 2001/HEALTH/conditions/10/15/ anthrax.butler).

Rosenberg, Barbara Hatch. "Analysis of Anthrax Attacks." Federation of American Scientists Web site. 2002. Retrieved April 10, 2002 (http://www.fas.org/bwc/ news/anthraxreport.htm).

Thompson, Mark, and Viveca Novak. "Tracking the Anthrax Attacks." CNN.com. Retrieved April 10, 2002 (http://www.cnn.com/ALLPOLITICS/time/2002/04/08/ anthrax.html).

INDEX

About the Author

Tahara Hasan is a freelance writer, graphic designer and illustrator. She is a graduate of Syracuse University. Her hobbies include watching Yankee baseball, spending time with her nephew Samuel, and baking pies with Mark P. Anderson.

Photo Credits

Cover, pp. 6, 46–47, 53 © AFP/Corbis; p. 5 © Joan Ryder, Gallo Images/Corbis; pp. 8–9, 14, 50, 51, 55 © Reuters NewMedia, Inc./Corbis; p. 12 © Scott Camazine/Photo Researchers, Inc.; pp. 15, 16–17, 19, 21, 24, 26–27, 28, 30, 32, 34–35, 37, 39, 41, 44, 48, 49 © AP/Wide World Photos.

Editor

Christine Poolos

Series Design and Layout

Geri Giordano